The Stronghold of Jezebel

A True Story of a Man's Journey

© 2016 by Bill Vincent.

All rights reserved. No part of this book may be reproduced, stored in a retrieval system or transmitted in any form or by any means without the prior written permission of the publishers, except by a reviewer who may quote brief passages in a review to be printed in a newspaper, magazine or journal.

Softcover 978-1-60796-980-8

PUBLISHED BY REVIVAL WAVES OF GLORY BOOKS & PUBLISHING
www.revivalwavesofgloryministries.com
Litchfield, IL

Printed in the United States of America

A True Story of a Man's Journey

The Stronghold of Jezebel

A True Story of a Man's Journey

By Bill Vincent

A True Story of a Man's Journey

Table of Contents

Introduction 5
The Jezebel Spirit 7
In the Beginning 28
The Wedding 31
The Ministry 33
The End of Jezebel's Reign 39
Characteristics of Jezebel 46
Happily Ever After 53
About the Author 55
Recommended Books 56

A True Story of a Man's Journey

Introduction

This is a book that God has laid on my heart for some time now. I believe that both men and women have first hand dealt with a spirit called Jezebel. I'm talking about more than just a distant spirit in the Church but actually married to this foul spirit.

This is a true story of my personal life. I really was married to a woman with a Jezebel spirit. I will tell you the story but will omit the names of people because we don't deal with flesh and blood but Principalities and Powers of wickedness in high places.

I will start out this book with a chapter that gives some scriptural basis on the spirit of Jezebel and characteristics of this spirit. Then I will write the story referring too many if not all of the characteristics of the Jezebel spirit.

A True Story of a Man's Journey

I know some people will really get stirred up and lash out at me but until you walk a mile in my shoes who are you to judge. This book will be controversial and if you know me at all I thrive in controversy. It has been about eighteen months since I left Jezebel. I am not writing this to vent or to put a person down. This book is to be a help to somebody if you have someone close to you consumed by a spirit you may need to cut it off to survive.

The Jezebel Spirit

This Chapter is to give some scriptural basis and characteristics of the Jezebel Spirit. There has been the restoration of the true Prophets of God. At the same time there has been a rise of false prophets, Jezebel and witchcraft. The enemy has assignments to kill God's true Prophets. We are going to begin to break every assignment and curse against God's true Prophets

Amos 3:7 Surely the Lord GOD will do nothing, but he revealeth his secret unto his servants the prophets.

But he revealeth his secret unto his servants the prophets. They are in strict correspondence with him, and he shows them things to come. Such secrets of God are revealed to them, that they may inform the people; that, by repentance and conversion, they may avoid the evil, and, by walking closely with God, secure the continuance of his favor.

First let's take a look at false Prophets

"Not everyone who says Lord, Lord is of God."

Matthew 7:15-18 Beware of false prophets, which come to you in sheep's clothing, but inwardly they are ravening wolves. Ye shall know them by their fruits. Do men gather grapes of thorns, or figs of thistles? Even so every good tree bringeth forth good fruit; but a corrupt tree bringeth forth evil fruit. A good tree cannot bring forth evil fruit, neither *can* a corrupt tree bring forth good fruit.

Jeremiah 23:25-27 I have heard what the prophets said, that prophesy lies in my name, saying, I have dreamed, I have dreamed. How long shall *this* be in the heart of the prophets that prophesy lies? Yea, *they are* prophets of the deceit of their own heart; Which think to cause my people to forget my name by their dreams which they tell every man to his neighbour, as their fathers have forgotten my name for Baal.

False Prophets using a spirit of witchcraft,

Jeremiah 27:9, 10 Therefore hearken not ye to your prophets, nor to your diviners, nor to your dreamers, nor to your enchanters, nor to your sorcerers, which speak unto you, saying, Ye shall not serve the king of Babylon: For they prophesy a lie unto you, to remove you far from your land; and that I should drive you out, and ye should perish.

Matthew 24:11 And many false prophets shall rise, and shall deceive many.

Matthew 24:24 For there shall arise false Christs, and false prophets, and shall shew great signs and wonders; insomuch that, if *it were* possible, they shall deceive the very elect.

Mark 13:22 For false Christs and false prophets shall rise, and shall shew signs and wonders, to seduce, if *it were* possible, even the elect.

Many would prefer to hear a false Prophet.....

2 Timothy 4:2-4 Preach the word; be instant in season, out of season; reprove, rebuke, exhort with all longsuffering and doctrine. For the time will come when they will not endure sound doctrine; but after their own lusts shall they heap to themselves teachers, having itching ears; And they shall turn away *their* ears from the truth, and shall be turned unto fables.

2 Timothy 2:1-3 Thou therefore, my son, be strong in the grace that is in Christ Jesus. And the things that thou hast heard of me among many witnesses, the same commit thou to faithful men, who shall be able to teach others also. Thou therefore endure hardness, as a good soldier of Jesus Christ.

False Prophets all seem to have a problem with Covetousness.

COVETOUSNESS MEANS,

1. A strong or inordinate desire of obtaining and possessing some supposed good; usually in a bad sense, and applied to an inordinate desire of wealth or avarice.

Out of the heart proceedeth covetousness. Mortify your members and covetousness which is idolatry.

2. Strong desire; eagerness.

True Prophets are in harmony with other True Prophets of God.

Some Characteristics of a false Prophet ..... They may have some or many of these characteristics,

They have a lying spirit

They use the Word for personal gain.

They rebel against authority

They have a controlling spirit

They speak what the pastors want to hear.

True prophets have to speak only what the Holy Spirit has given to them.

They are after money..... (much like taking offerings for miracles.) There are those that will take offerings and misuse scripture to get money.

Let's now look at Jezebel,

They may have some or many of these characteristics,

They are out to kill the true prophets and stop them from assuming their proper position in the Church. (They hate the true prophet in fear of being exposed.)

They go after the position of the true prophet.

They stir and manipulate.

They are a major part of establishing false prophets

They rebel.... This is the sin of witchcraft.

A True Story of a Man's Journey

They have hatred vengeance and murder. (One of the definitions of murder is to destroy someone's reputation.) That Jezebel will attempt to do to those whom have seen there true colors.

They have a lying spirit.

Jezebel can be a man or a woman

They stir and manipulate their spouse.

If Jezebel is not already in Leadership they will always seek to be positioned in Leadership.

Witchcraft is in use by Jezebel

They have a controlling spirit

They don't do what is right in the sight of God but what is right in their own eyes.

They accuse True Prophets of not speaking the complete true Word of the Lord.

Jezebel has a seducing spirit and it attaches itself to the body of Christ like a virus.

They want to become the center of worship and/or the center of attention.

They demand obedience to their every command.

Jezebel uses familiar spirits to prophesy.

They have Intimidation, pride; hate, won't submit (but appears to be submitted.) and they sow discord.

They undermine authority

They are religious (appears to be loyal, faithful, but only to accomplish its purpose.)

They cannot admit wrong. It's always someone else's fault.

False humility

Considers themselves to be important

Now let's look more at Witchcraft and it's characteristics that may be in the Church,

Sorcery

Divination by assistance of evil spirits Witchcraft always is controlling.

It denies everything that Jesus has purchased for us.

Witchcraft and a Controlling Spirit are one in the same.

Independence (or rebelling against authority) in a believer may have been infected with this spirit of witchcraft.

There are believers who have used their liberty in Christ and use that freedom as their defense in rebellion. It is about the attitude of the heart.

We must have a heart to obey God's Word and walk in liberty without rebelling.

We must examine our hearts and motives and be able to discern. We can accomplish this by sincerely submitting to someone we can trust that has discernment of the Spirit of the Lord.

A True Story of a Man's Journey

Witchcraft Spirit is active in the false Prophet and Jezebel and has caused pastors to fear the true Prophets.

When we are dealing with the False Prophet, Jezebel and Witchcraft... We are dealing with Baal.

Here are some things to consider concerning Baal,

Baal is a false god.

This false god gives false peace of prosperity then destroys any one who serves him.

The name Baal roughly means "The Storm god"

Baal is a weather and fertility god.

God spoke this to me. When dealing with the false god Baal you are dealing with a swarming dense spirit in the atmosphere.

You can expect some dark moods in the spirit and stormy spiritual seasons.

Baal is known also as the god of wealth

Jezebels death,

2 Kings 9:33 And he said, Throw her down. So they threw her down: and *some* of her blood was sprinkled on the wall, and on the horses: and he trode her under foot.

No mercy on Jezebel.

Baal, Witchcraft, false prophets and jezebel have many spirits compiled in their evil destructive ways.

2 Kings 10:26-28 And they brought forth the images out of the house of Baal, and burned them. And they brake down the image of Baal, and brake down the house of Baal, and made it a draught house unto this day. Thus Jehu destroyed Baal out of Israel.

It takes the anointing of God to destroy Ahab, Jezebel, False Prophets, Witchcraft and Baal.

We cannot allow these Spirits to come in and control our Churches and our lives.

2 Thessalonians 2:9-12 *Even him,* whose coming is after the working of Satan with all power and signs and lying wonders, And with all deceivableness of unrighteousness in them that perish; because they received not the love of the truth, that they might be saved. And for this cause God shall send them strong delusion, that they should believe a lie: That they all might be damned who believed not the truth, but had pleasure in unrighteousness.

Micah 5:11-13 And I will cut off the cities of thy land, and throw down all thy strong holds: And I will cut off witchcrafts out of thine hand; and thou shalt have no *more* soothsayers: Thy graven images also will I cut off, and thy standing images out of the midst of thee; and thou shalt no more worship the work of thine hands.

Whenever an individual or Church becomes prophetic, the devil will send a jezebel spirit to try and stop them. If a Church is going after the supernatural, this spirit will attempt to come to destroy that which God is doing.

A True Story of a Man's Journey

Jezebel means,

According to the Old Testament, she encouraged idolatry…. A woman who is regarded as evil and scheming….

According to the *Bible* the wicked woman who married Ahab, king of Israel…. Any woman regarded as shameless and wicked.

I believe this spirit can be on women, men or even a couple. Here are some things Jezebel is known by,

Jezebel Killed God's Prophets, Worshiped Baal, had sexual immoralities like orgies, Controlling Ahab (husband) threatening letters to Prophets, Control through fear and deception and wrote letters in her husband's name.

We have been commanded to cast out devils.

Luke 10:17 And the seventy returned again with joy, saying, Lord, even the devils are subject unto us through thy name.

Matthew 16:17 And Jesus answered and said unto him, Blessed art thou, Simon Barjona: for flesh and blood hath not revealed *it* unto thee, but my Father which is in heaven.

Revelations 2:20-22 Notwithstanding I have a few things against thee, because thou sufferest that woman Jezebel, which calleth herself a prophetess, to teach and to seduce my servants to commit fornication, and to eat things sacrificed unto idols. And I gave her space to repent of her fornication; and she repented not. Behold, I will cast her into a bed, and them that commit adultery with her into great tribulation, except they repent of their deeds.

Spirit of Jezebel will try to control

Jezebel can manifest through a man or a woman. This spirit mostly originates from controlling or being controlled.

This Spirit controls people through intimidation and fear. It wants to get into positions of authority.

The spirit can even be upon couples. Initially they can be tremendous, faithful people, attending all the meetings, working to fully support the vision and offering themselves as volunteers.

They support with their lips, but their heart is far from you. After a while, they start to talk to people of influence in the congregation, (I'm concerned about the Pastors, the leaders, about the finances and the way the things are done.)

Jezebel is a two faced spirit

Jezebel comes from two different words. In the Old Testament they are, friend or companion on the one side, murderer on the other.

In the New Testament, it also has two words, Chaste (means: not indulging in unlawful sexual activity; virtuous…. Sexually abstinent; celibate…. Pure, decent, or modest in nature, behavior, etc.) and continually sinful on the other.

When you feel something wrong, most other people that you may ask would say. (NOT THEM! THEY ARE SUCH LOVELY PEOPLE)

Jezebel spirit's secret weapon is when confronted; they will deny and make you feel like something is wrong with you.

Jezebel yields to no one

Jezebel also means without co-habitation, Refuses to co-habit with people unless they are in control.

Jezebel is attracted to weak people

Ahab was a weak leader. If any one with a Jezebel Spirit is married, they are in charge.

Revelations 2:20 Notwithstanding I have a few things against thee, because thou sufferest that woman Jezebel, which calleth herself a prophetess, to teach and to seduce my servants to commit fornication, and to eat things sacrificed unto idols.

God didn't call her she called herself.

A True Story of a Man's Journey

Signs of a Jezebel

You feel intimidated to spend money, and you are the boss.

You are afraid to speak to a leader and yet people are complaining about them and they are going through workers like their going out of style. They are (takeovers) happening in your leadership and it's the same person taking everything over.

You cannot spontaneously do anything without having to ask this person's opinion first.

You are discouraged and depressed and are considering leaving the ministry, your spouse or life itself.

Characteristics of a Jezebel Spirit
Hates authority

Jezebel loves to be honored but honors no one.

Control

A True Story of a Man's Journey

If they are submissive they only do it to gain control. They can never be satisfied, give them one area and they will want more and more. It is like a drug to them. They want to control the finances. Whoever controls the finances, controls the vision.

They control the flow of the Holy Spirit.

When the Jezebel Spirit is in the house, the righteous, peace and joy that should be there, becomes confusion, disharmony and a striving spirit. When they leave tithes are up, souls are coming back and God moves mightily.

Brings a striving spirit

A striving spirit is to lead ministers to burnout. It can cause leaders to strive for money and numbers that leads to nothing but destruction.

Drove Elijah to the edge

It brings accusations and criticism that makes the leader want to die.

Has a spirit of lust that operates through them.

Jezebel was sensual and used it to control and manipulate.

How has it entered, in the first place

Exodus 20:5 Thou shalt not bow down thyself to them, nor serve them: for I the LORD thy God *am* a jealous God, visiting the iniquity **of the fathers upon the children unto the third and fourth *generation*** of them that hate me;

How do we get a person free?

John 20:23 Whose soever sins ye remit, they are remitted unto them; *and* whose soever *sins* ye retain, they are retained.

(If you forgive the sins of any they are forgiven, if you retain the sins of any they are retained.)

This means if you repent of sin in your parents and grandparents and turn from their sins, you have to let go of their sins, but if you don't do that you have retained them.

Galatians 3:13 Christ hath redeemed us from the curse of the law, being made a curse for us: for it is written, Cursed *is* every one that hangeth on a tree:

REPENTANCE

How to deliver your Church?

Jezebel hates the Prophets because they speak the Word of the Lord. It hates prayer because prayer binds it.

Four steps to victory

1. Personal confrontation

Matthew 18:15 Moreover if thy brother shall trespass against thee, go and tell him his fault between thee and him alone: if he shall hear thee, thou hast gained thy brother.

2. Take witnesses to the confrontation

Matthew 18:16 But if he will not hear *thee, then* take with thee one or two more, that in the mouth of two or three witnesses every word may be established.

3. Take it to the Church

Matthew 18:17 And if he shall neglect to hear them, tell *it* unto the church: but if he neglect to hear the church, let him be unto thee as an heathen man and a publican.

4. God will honor the decision in heaven

Matthew 18:18 Verily I say unto you, Whatsoever ye shall bind on earth shall be bound in heaven: and whatsoever ye shall loose on earth shall be loosed in heaven.

A True Story of a Man's Journey

In the Beginning

I was raised up in a world of hard times. I was just seventeen when the relationship started. I don't believe she had the spirit of Jezebel then but I know it wasn't long after. I had just got saved and the woman that became my wife was influenced by the spirit of Jezebel, she was indeed a major part of getting me saved.

I was at a place of gratitude of getting me out of a life of drugs and alcohol that I looked to this woman in a way that was not good. I remember that I was walking home and began to feel these feelings that I believe now to be do to a seducing spirit. I even bound the enemy that day when I felt those feelings and she convinced me that the feelings was of God even though she was married to another man at the time. The relationship went for five to six years before marriage. During that time she divorced her husband and the woman did help me get a job and to have some kind of life.

There were times that the influence of the Jezebel spirit was strong and other times it didn't seem like it was there. If there was a time that I began to feel that I was being controlled by her then the spirit would lay low.

Now I want you to know that during the early years and even later I dealt with a lot of evil spirits apart from the spirit of Jezebel that was in her. I was raised in a life of deceit, lust and robbing to get ahead. You need to understand that I'm exposing myself to let people know that to become a preacher of revival, with healing, miracles, signs and wonders, God has worked with me and made me that man of God. It is after many failures and shortcomings. Out of all that I dealt with there was nothing as strong as the spirit of Jezebel that nearly killed me as a man of God.

A True Story of a Man's Journey

Have you ever heard what doesn't kill us will make us stronger. I have to tell you that now I have been used to deliver over a thousand people and I know it's because of the Holy Spirit. He still has taught me through much of my life. See I had been married to Jezebel for thirteen years and in a relationship for a total of nineteen years. This woman with the spirit of Jezebel had been in my life almost as long as Jesus has been in my heart. I have had to be pushed down, put down in front of others and to feel defeated and still blessed by God in the midst of it. God has made me a man of God despite much of the continuous battles.

A True Story of a Man's Journey

The Wedding

After being in a relationship for years we married. It was in a little home and a private wedding. We married and I knew that it was odd not to have any family or friends but again she convinced me that was okay. Another thing that puzzled me was that we never consummated the marriage as most couples do on their wedding night.

This marriage was always binding to me. I would always have a new restricted area in my life. Understand I did my share of sinful mistakes but I was constantly put down. Being married to a person with a Jezebel spirit is like a strict mother that has evil intentions. Soon after being married she had us keep it a secret from her family and if she saw someone she knew it was like she didn't know who I was.

It was a couple of years before there was any real acknowledging me as her husband. I know now that was because God really poured out His anointing on my life. I began to prophesy and preach and the anointing of God got stronger and stronger. This was when the strong beginning of that evil spirit Jezebel in her life. She got stronger when the call of a Prophet of God came on my life.

This marriage was not a normal marriage at all. Being married for thirteen years there was no sex for over ten of those years.

A True Story of a Man's Journey

The Ministry

Many years into the marriage we began to travel for ministry and then ended in being Pastors of a Church. God always will do good to them who love Him. God brought me to heights I never dreamed of and it was in the midst of the highest reign of Jezebel. It was as if we both were hitting new levels.

I know that deep down this woman consumed by the Jezebel spirit loved God. She loved the higher levels of Glory but somewhere she got off line. I know it was because of that spirit in her wanted to be lifted up and enjoyed it. The Church we had was not dead in any way. We had a large group of hungry people and we were blessed. Before I talk about that part of the ministry, let me go back closer to the beginning.

In the beginning of the ministry we truly struggled and I learned much. First off we will begin when we stepped out into full time ministry. When we incorporated the ministry she convinced me that she should be the President and I would be Vice-President. She wanted control and she used that position to keep that control.

Some may say that I just had a controlling wife. I want you to know that the difference between a controlling wife and a wife that is Jezebel.... The controlling wife is just that controlling. The Jezebel spirit uses witchcraft, control, manipulation and familiar spirits.

When the Ministry began to bring in money it was time to get paid for the work of the Ministry. She convinced me again that even though I was the one that traveled, spoke and ran the every day ministry that she should be the one to receive a salary. So for four years she received a salary and I didn't receive a dime. You may say well she was your wife but.... Any one who works hard should receive payment. It is a real slap in the face. Even after four years when I finally received a salary it was at the starter salary. For the entire marriage I was to give my entire check over to her as soon as I got it. Jezebel always controls the money. Every decision had to be to her approval and she kept a tight reign on those decisions.

One thing that I didn't see until I left was all the hurt people. If anyone got in Jezebels way or was drawn to me more than her, it was time to cut them off. She would ban people from Church and even cut people off and I know it hurt some people. After my eyes were open to this I cried many tears of sorrow. No one should ever be banned from Church to receive. Every time I would start to get acknowledged she would cut them off because she should be the center. Jezebel will always justify all the carnage they leave behind.

By the time we became Pastors she really grew to be the strongest. One thing people did unaware was to lift Jezebel up into her ultimate reign. There was always women surrounding her and she had them even confirming every bit of her hurting and bringing destruction to anyone whom saw her as she was or got close to me. There were many late night gossip sessions she led. It got to the point if Jezebel said anything it would be backed by all or else. She would sit in the sound booth and then there was a gathering around her. Signs and wonders would manifest in our meetings and she would just gleam as she looked at them. She didn't want anyone to have them but her. The thing is that every meeting that the signs would come she would hold them for all to see and then the presence of God died. God was no longer the center. Night after night people came and the meetings had never been better and after Jezebel and I was led into the dining room. I would get told how she didn't have enough attention and how I messed up the meeting. This happened probably ninety percent of the time. As soon as someone walked in she would say be quiet. She didn't want people to see her true colors. If people would tell me how great the meeting was she would just glare at me and pull out the signs and wonders that came in the meeting and then she was surrounded.

She got to the place that controlling my life wasn't enough she had to control many. People wouldn't even make basic decisions without her approval. One woman wasn't allowed to hang out with anyone because Jezebel told her not to. I'm talking about even people that were part of our team of Ministry. This woman was the last one that remained under her rule after I left. (God please help her)

Jezebel even had the entire Church convinced that we should pray against another Church. There was a Church whom did attack me personal from her own Ministry but Jezebel held special meetings to pray against that Ministry from getting a building. This is witchcraft no matter how you look at it. This went on for months. This was just one of many meetings against something or someone.

This is what a person with the Jezebel Spirit does. They will start at their home and then to the Church until they reach the top or destroy the Church which ever. Lastly the spirit will

A True Story of a Man's Journey

begin to merge its poison to other Churches and cities.

A True Story of a Man's Journey

The End of Jezebel's Reign

After Jezebel was put at her highest reign, God had a plan to dethrone her. At the time I had spent hours seeking the Lord concerning the way I was feeling. I would get lifted up by the Lord and tore down by Jezebel. We were in the midst of Revival that had continued two years straight. There were times I would tell the Lord when the Revival ends I can just leave and keep everyone happy.

There was about a month before I left where God did more miracles than ever. People were healed of various cancers and other tangible miracles. It was awesome but at the same time horrible as far as my personal life. God spoke and said that we were to have a special Cast-Out Devil's Conference on a Thursday night. Unknown to me that the weekend after would be my last weekend there. You would think a Cast-Out Devil's Conference would be a strong title for a conference but we were packed. God had told me that He would tell me the right time to go. That Thursday night devils were cast out by the many. God anointed me that night to give demons the count of three and five to leave and they did. People were squirming like snakes on the ground. Jezebel would try to stir up people whom had already been delivered with no success. Jezebel would attempt to stay close to me to have the appearance of being used of God. At the end of that meeting Jezebel was standing in the isle and I asked her if she needed anything and she responded NO!!! I believe that was her last chance to keep Revival. After the meeting Jezebel was so upset because of the way God had anointed me and took the spotlight off of her.

God spoke that the Saturday night would be a Grand Finale. Friday night was awesome one of the best meetings I've ever been in but no comparison to Saturday night. There were more signs and wonders that night than any time in the revival. There were people being hit with God's Glory at another level.

We had a guest speaker Sunday and the meeting was so heavy. There was no anointing and Spirit moving. After the meeting I began to tell Jezebel something just didn't feel right. I heard the sweetest word for the Lord GO!!! Wow it was awesome I knew I was leaving and I told Jezebel I was leaving. She said let me have some of the team pray for me. So I agreed to stay until the next day. Jezebel told my own team I wanted to leave because I had demons and she also convinced them that I was leaving for another woman in the Church. For hours I was being attacked verbally about leaving and regarding this other woman. See it was no longer anything wrong with her but me and others. After a while I contacted the woman they were speaking to me about and asked her if she would leave, because I was leaving with or without her. She said if you go I go. She had two children and the way these so called Christians were acting it would have scared them for life. Finally I ran in my office loaded an

A True Story of a Man's Journey

empty box with clothes and ran out the door with Jezebel screaming he's leaving. I ran down the hall with three ladies chasing me. I got in my old van and they were jumping in to stop me from leaving. After a while they knew they were not stopping me. I left and swung around the corner and picked up the woman they were talking about. Was this ideal NO but you don't know what you would do until you are chased by some Christians. As soon as we drove away my eyes were open to everything. I saw all that Jezebel had done. Next thing, we had multiple cars chasing us. Yes, we had a Jezebel car chase. Finally we got away after some time. It is noted of how it looked but I knew God said GO!!!

After we had left the rumors started, I left the Ministry for another woman. The truth is I left Jezebel and so did another woman. There was one of my right hand ministry team women I talked to after I had left and she said with her own mouth that my wife at the time was jezebel. Another woman from the ministry came up to my vehicle and said all that was done against me was wrong.

See Jezebel got the Church Team members to pray witchcraft prayers against me and anyone who left. When I left it caused the wrath of Jezebel to come forth and she was exposing herself. One person after they left told me of the twenty four hour prayer to get me back. The prayers had things like for me not to have any money, breaking of relationships etc. There was also a time she said that Jezebel did a spell with salt and pepper. She had me fired two days after I had left from the Ministry. She gave an appearance that she wanted me back but this was a lie too.

God knew how things would cause Jezebel to explode and reveal her true colors. This was the beginning of many people's eyes being opened. The Revival continued with much secrecy concerning my reason for leaving. They were telling people that I had a family emergency.

The lies, manipulation and witchcraft continued. There were rumors of me leaving the ministry and having affairs with multiple women, all untrue. They found where I lived and drove by praying against me multiple times a day. I indeed became Jezebel's enemy and so did anyone who left her side. The Revival did end after things caught up with Jezebel. Many said I killed Revival but the truth is God said Grand Finale. God ended it that day and began to dethrone Jezebel's Kingdom. I had to lay my life down so she would fall.

I know to this day I could have done things different but I did do right. I received a prophetic Word from a Prophet after I left that said Jezebel was sucking the very life out of me. He said I had to leave to live. I contacted a lawyer about divorcing her. Since she didn't want to change I had to divorce the woman whom was Jezebel. Well she even wanted to have control of that too. God told me not to fight for anything so I released five automobiles the ministry and five homes. She wanted to be the one who filed for the divorce. So I let her and she filed in a different county so no one would know she filed and got all but one old van. She wanted to keep

A True Story of a Man's Journey

the poor woman whom had her husband leave her for another woman. This was a façade she wanted to keep to get sympathy. The divorce was done about five weeks after I had left.

The Church that I left is now an empty building. I don't like that part but I also thought me being the prophetic man of God that people would have listened to me instead of Jezebel.

A True Story of a Man's Journey

Characteristics of Jezebel

Here are some of the characteristics of Jezebel that this woman carried. I will list the characteristic with a description of how she was infected.

They are out to kill the true prophets and stop them from assuming their proper position in the Church. (They hate the true prophet in fear of being exposed.)

This woman was little by little killing me. After my eyes were open I saw her as she was I became the enemy. She was out to destroy me but thanks to God she was not able.

A True Story of a Man's Journey

They go after the position of the true prophet.

She was going after my own position to be the prophetic voice that the Church listened to.

They stir and manipulate.

She was stirring all who surrounded themselves around her. There was always a enemy of some person that she convinced all who followed her, to pray against.

They have hatred vengeance and murder. (One of the definitions of murder is to destroy someone's reputation.) That Jezebel will attempt to do to those whom have seen there true colors.

Every person whom would attempt to leave the Church she would murder their reputation. She did this with me leaving. She started many rumors even that the woman accused of having an affair with was pregnant with my baby. To this day that woman still has not been pregnant let alone with my baby.

They have a lying spirit.

If you say something that is false or make up something that isn't true, it's a lie. This woman was notorious for making up things about people.

They stir and manipulate their spouse.

This was true. She had a way to convince me that what she did was always right. If she had us pray against another ministry she had a way to get you to agree and if you didn't you were next on her hit list.

Witchcraft is in use by Jezebel

Praying for bad things to happen to other Christians is witchcraft. This woman did this on many occasions toward anyone who was considered her enemy. It was reported to me by people she had prayed specific prayers against me.

They have a controlling spirit

She had to be the one in control of all decisions made in the ministry. After that she began to control people in the congregation and then her own mother she controls her finances and decisions.

They don't do what is right in the sight of God but what is right in their own eyes.

She had the ability to convince people that what she did was right even if it was contrary to God and His Word.

They accuse True Prophets of not speaking the complete true Word of the Lord.

If a Prophet spoke anything that she didn't like she would begin to tear apart the Words. This was even true with my Words I spoke in the last month before I left. She convinced all who were left that it wasn't the true Word of God.

Jezebel has a seducing spirit and it attaches itself to the body of Christ like a virus.

It got to the point that every member got wrapped around Jezebels little finger. Some people couldn't even pay bills without checking with her first.

They want to become the center of worship and/or the center of attention.

She had to control the music and worship. She didn't want anyone to know the artists of the songs or nothing. She would turn the entire worship team's microphones way down so hers was the loudest.

They demand obedience to their every command.

If she called you had to come or you were off the team. If you didn't respond with obedience you were off the team.

Jezebel uses familiar spirits to prophesy.

She would talk to people and prophesy things she learned through conversations.

They have Intimidation, pride; hate, won't submit (but appears to be submitted.) and they sow discord.

This was all true for this woman. She was consumed with all these things. She had intimidation to the point you would think something was wrong with you. She thought so high of herself that she could do no wrong. She had hate for anyone who left the Church or saw her as she really was. She would only submit if she was in charge and sowing discord to separate any one whom were closer friends than with her. There were two women if they got close at all she would talk bad about one to get them to separate.

A True Story of a Man's Journey

They cannot admit wrong. It's always someone else's fault.

She never did anything wrong and if you thought she did, she made you feel guilty of wrong.

Jezebel is attracted to weak people

When we met I was a weak man. She would always control weak people.

A True Story of a Man's Journey

Happily Ever After

After leaving Jezebel to destroy herself through her own hateful plans, we finally got to live free. You don't know how awesome it is to get from under that control. I am now remarried to a wonderful woman with two girls. I finally have had the joy of have a baby girl. I know what a real marriage is like now. It's a give and take relationship with God the center of all you do. I have a ministry that is flourishing and despite all the lies she spoke against me it is all good. People have slowly here and there come to the meetings because it is true you know them by their fruit. People are seeing that even though I left in a controversial way that God has redeemed me. Even if any of the rumors had been true they seem to forget the awesome mercy of salvation and repentance. God is truly

A True Story of a Man's Journey

faithful that when Jezebel tries to kill you and turn the Church against you He is always there with you.

A True Story of a Man's Journey

About the Author

Bill Vincent is no stranger to understanding the power of God. Not only has he spent over twenty years as a Minister with a strong prophetic anointing, he is now also an Apostle and Author with Revival Waves of Glory Ministries in Litchfield, IL. Along with his wife, Tabitha, he, leads a team providing apostolic oversight in all aspects of ministry, including service, personal ministry and Godly character.

Bill offers a wide range of writings and teachings from deliverance, to experiencing presence of God and developing Apostolic cutting edge Church structure. Drawing on the power of the Holy Spirit through years of experience in Revival, Spiritual Sensitivity, and deliverance ministry, Bill now focuses mainly on pursuing the Presence of God and breaking the power of the devil off of people's lives.

His books 48 and counting has since helped many people to overcome the spirits and curses of Satan. For more information or to keep up with Bill's latest releases, please visit www.revivalwavesofgloryministries.com. To contact Bill, feel free to follow him on twitter @revivalwaves.

A True Story of a Man's Journey

Recommended Books

By Bill Vincent
Overcoming Obstacles
Glory: Pursuing God's Presence
Defeating the Demonic Realm
Increasing Your Prophetic Gift
Increasing Your Anointing
Keys to Receiving Your Miracle
The Supernatural Realm
Waves of Revival
Increase of Revelation and Restoration
The Resurrection Power of God
Discerning Your Call of God
Apostolic Breakthrough
Glory: Increasing God's Presence
Love is Waiting – Don't Let Love Pass You By
The Healing Power of God
Glory: Expanding God's Presence
Receiving Personal Prophecy
Signs and Wonders
Signs and Wonders Revelations
Children Stories
The Rapture

A True Story of a Man's Journey

The Secret Place of God's Power
Building a Prototype Church
Breakthrough of Spiritual Strongholds
Glory: Revival Presence of God
Overcoming the Power of Lust
Glory: Kingdom Presence of God
Transitioning Into a Prototype Church
The Stronghold of Jezebel
Healing After Divorce
A Closer Relationship With God
Cover Up and Save Yourself
Desperate for God's Presence
The War for Spiritual Battles
Spiritual Leadership
Global Warning
Millions of Churches
Destroying the Jezebel Spirit
Awakening of Miracles
Deception and Consequences Revealed
Are You a Follower of Christ
Don't Let the Enemy Steal from You!
A Godly Shaking
The Unsearchable Riches of Christ
Heaven's Court System
Satan's Open Doors
Armed for Battle
The Wrestler
Spiritual Warfare: Complete Collection
Growing In the Prophetic
The Prototype Church: Complete Edition
Faith
The Rapture

A True Story of a Man's Journey

To Order:

Email:
rwgcontact@yahoo.com

Web Site:
www.revivalwavesofgloryministries.com

Mail Order:
Revival Waves of Glory
PO Box 596
Litchfield, IL 62056

Shipping $5.00
If you mail an order and pay by check, make check out to Revival Waves of Glory.

Most books are in multiple formats such as Hardcover, Soft-Cover, Ebook (such as Kindle & Nook), and Audio Books.

www.ingramcontent.com/pod-product-compliance
Lightning Source LLC
Chambersburg PA
CBHW052119070526
44584CB00017B/2562